Piano Duet Play·Along

VOLUME 6

1 PIANO, 4 HANDS

DISNEY SONGS

ISBN-13: 978-1-4234-2131-3
ISBN-10: 1-4234-2131-0

Walt Disney Music Company

Wonderland Music Company, Inc.

DISTRIBUTED BY

HAL•LEONARD®
CORPORATION

7777 W. BLUEMOUND RD. P.O. BOX 13819 MILWAUKEE, WI 53213

In Australia Contact:
Hal Leonard Australia Pty. Ltd.
4 Lentara Court
Cheltenham, Victoria, 3192 Australia
Email: ausadmin@halleonard.com

Visit Hal Leonard Online at
www.halleonard.com

CANDLE ON THE WATER

from Walt Disney's PETE'S DRAGON

SECONDO

Words and Music by AL KASHA
and JOEL HIRSCHHORN

CANDLE ON THE WATER

from Walt Disney's PETE'S DRAGON

PRIMO

Words and Music by AL KASHA
and JOEL HIRSCHHORN

Smoothly, with expression
Both hands 8va throughout

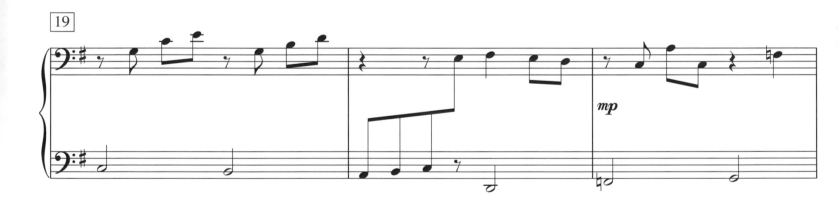

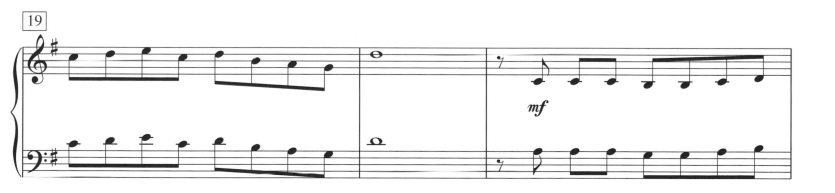

SECONDO

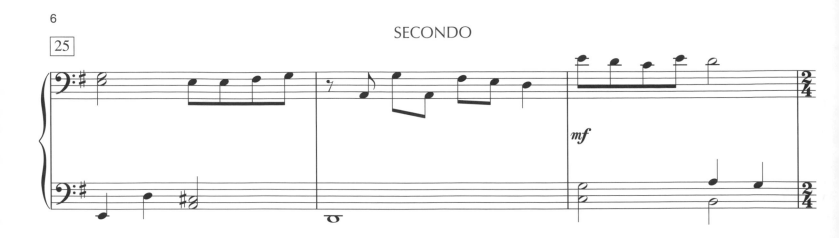

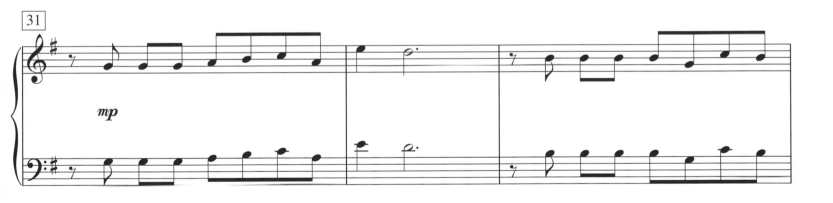

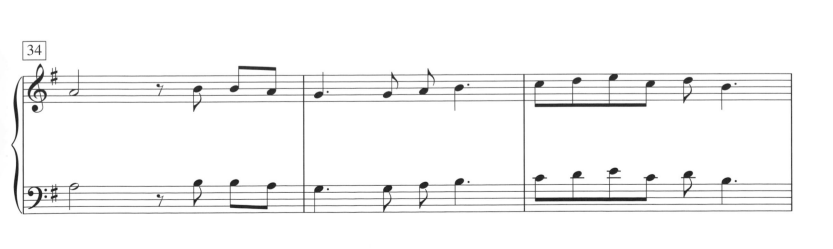

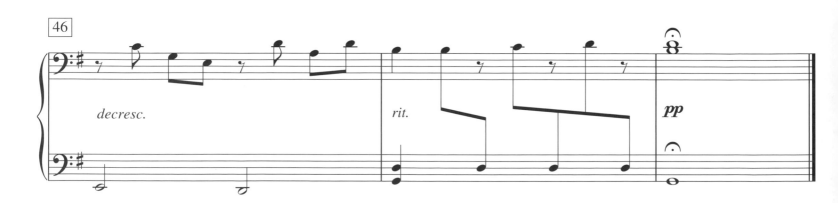

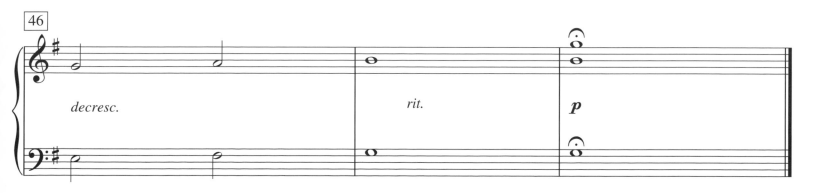

COLORS OF THE WIND
from Walt Disney's POCAHONTAS
SECONDO

Music by ALAN MENKEN
Lyrics by STEPHEN SCHWARTZ

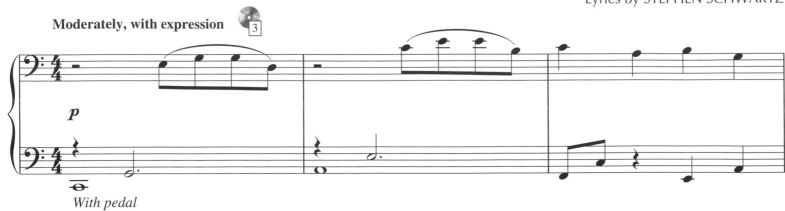

COLORS OF THE WIND
from Walt Disney's POCAHONTAS
PRIMO

Music by ALAN MENKEN
Lyrics by STEPHEN SCHWARTZ

Moderately, with expression

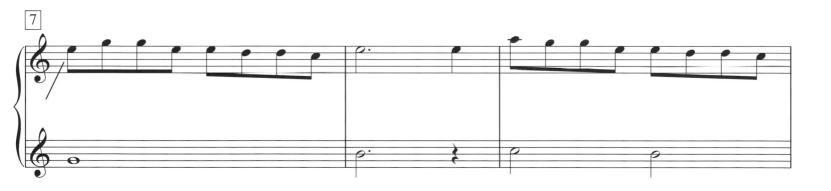

SECONDO

FEED THE BIRDS

from Walt Disney's MARY POPPINS

SECONDO

Words and Music by RICHARD M. SHERMAN
and ROBERT B. SHERMAN

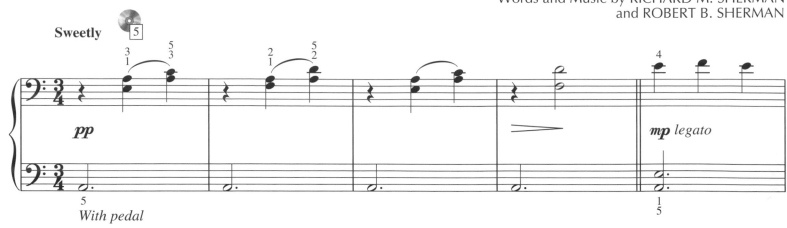

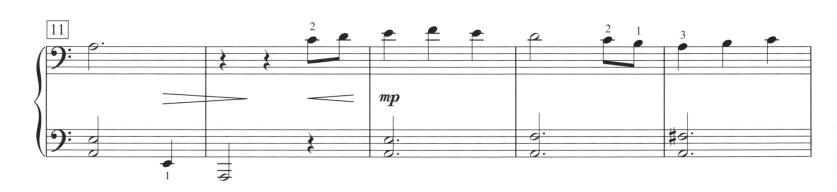

FEED THE BIRDS
from Walt Disney's MARY POPPINS

PRIMO

Words and Music by RICHARD M. SHERMAN
and ROBERT B. SHERMAN

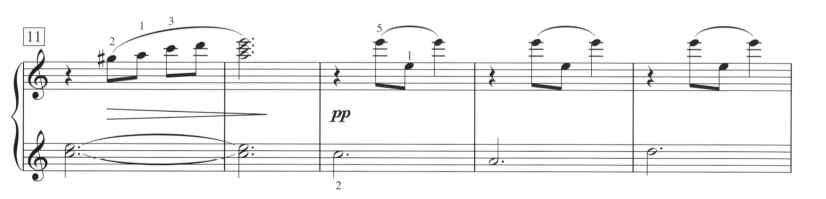

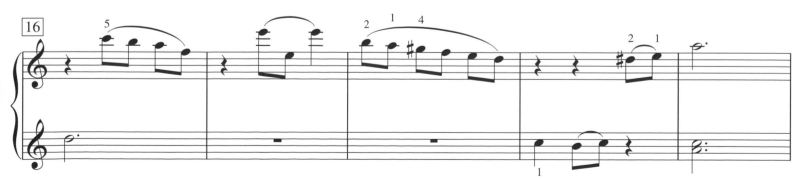

SECONDO

SECONDO

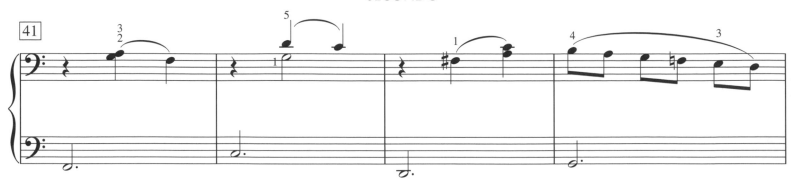

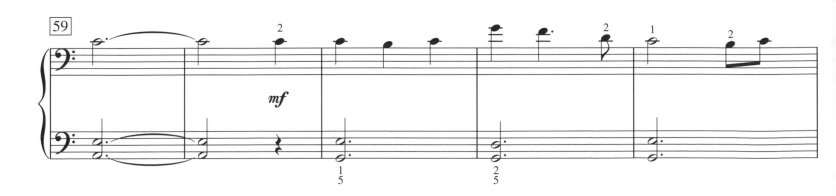

SECONDO

GO THE DISTANCE

from Walt Disney Pictures' HERCULES

SECONDO

Music by ALAN MENKEN
Lyrics by DAVID ZIPPEL

GO THE DISTANCE
from Walt Disney Pictures' HERCULES

PRIMO

Music by ALAN MENKEN
Lyrics by DAVID ZIPPEL

SECONDO

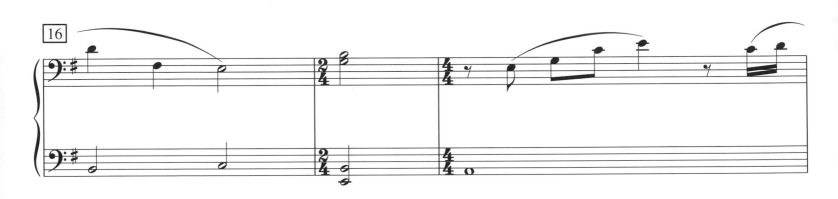

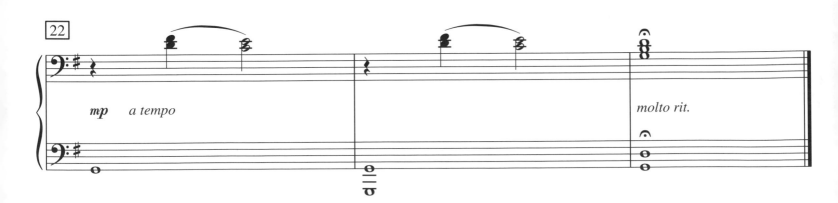

PRIMO

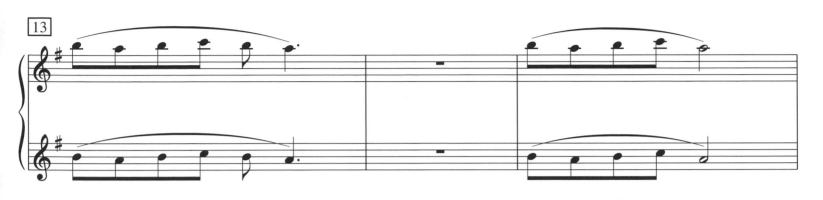

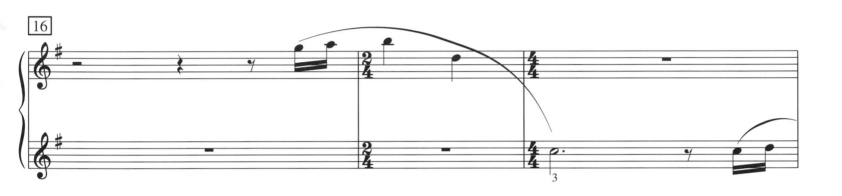

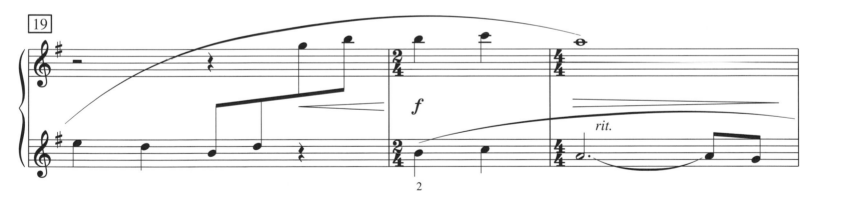

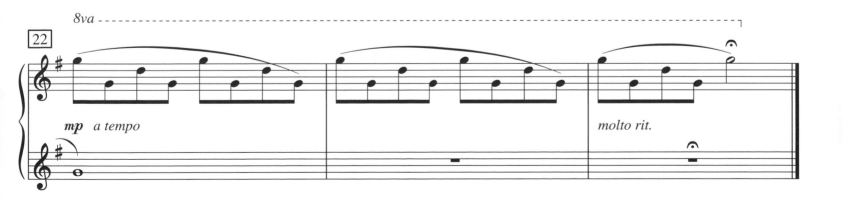

KISS THE GIRL
from Walt Disney's THE LITTLE MERMAID

SECONDO

Lyrics by HOWARD ASHMAN
Music by ALAN MENKEN

KISS THE GIRL
from Walt Disney's THE LITTLE MERMAID

PRIMO

Lyrics by HOWARD ASHMAN
Music by ALAN MENKEN

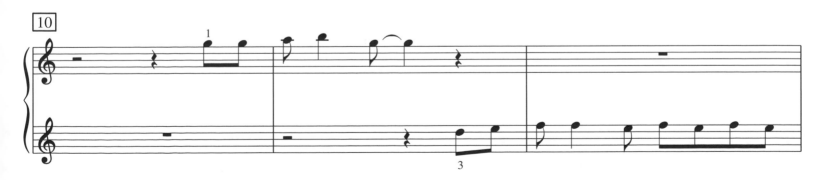

SECONDO

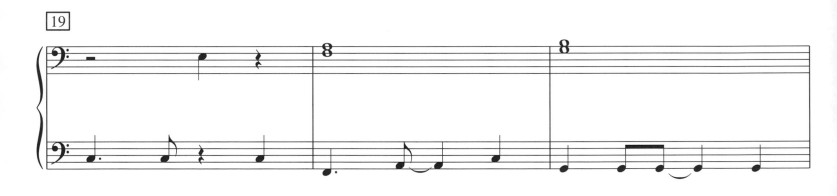

PRIMO

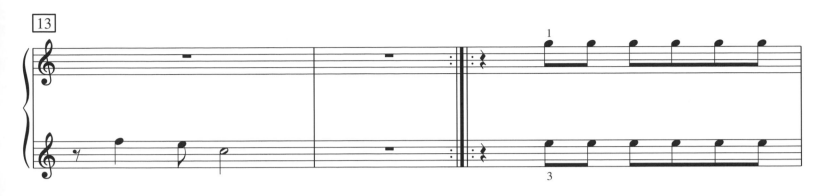

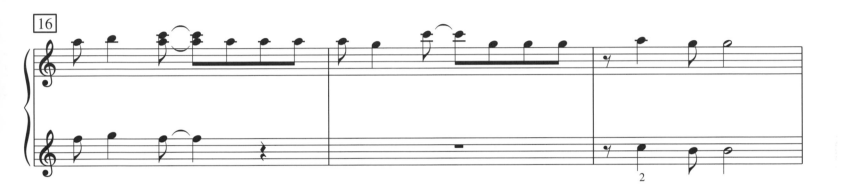

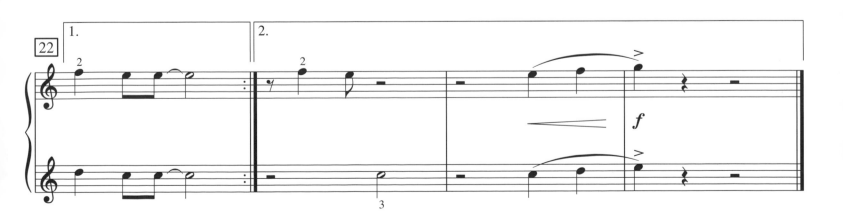

YOU'LL BE IN MY HEART

(Pop Version)
from Walt Disney Pictures' TARZAN ™

SECONDO

Words and Music by
PHIL COLLINS

YOU'LL BE IN MY HEART
(Pop Version)
from Walt Disney Pictures' TARZAN ™

PRIMO

Words and Music by
PHIL COLLINS

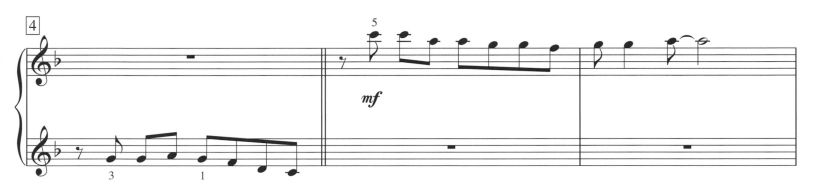

SECONDO

PRIMO

SECONDO

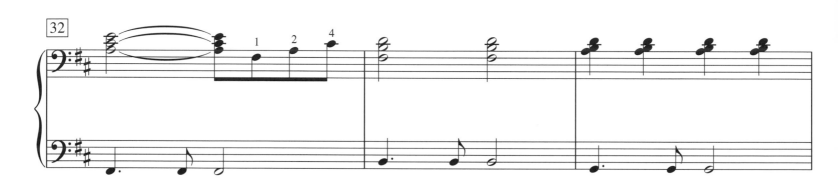

D.S. al Coda

CODA

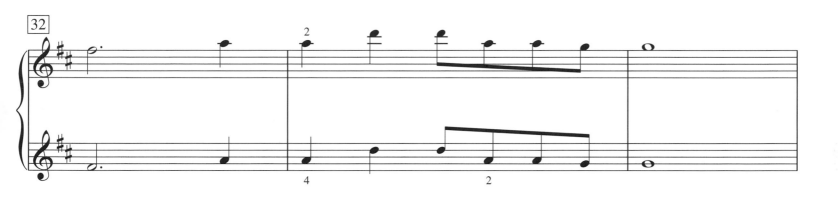

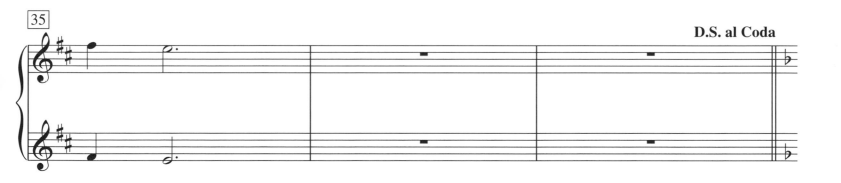

D.S. al Coda

CODA

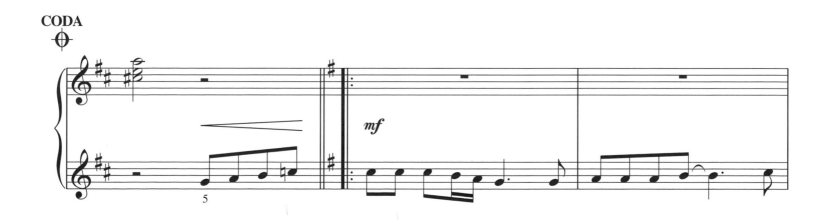

SECONDO

SECONDO

PRIMO

ZIP-A-DEE-DOO-DAH

from Walt Disney's SONG OF THE SOUTH
from Disneyland and Walt Disney World's SPLASH MOUNTAIN

SECONDO

Words by RAY GILBERT
Music by ALLIE WRUBEL

ZIP-A-DEE-DOO-DAH

from Walt Disney's SONG OF THE SOUTH
from Disneyland and Walt Disney World's SPLASH MOUNTAIN

PRIMO

Words by RAY GILBERT
Music by ALLIE WRUBEL

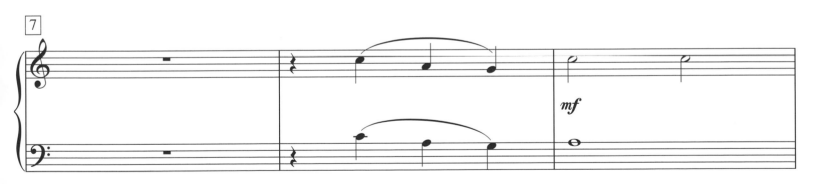

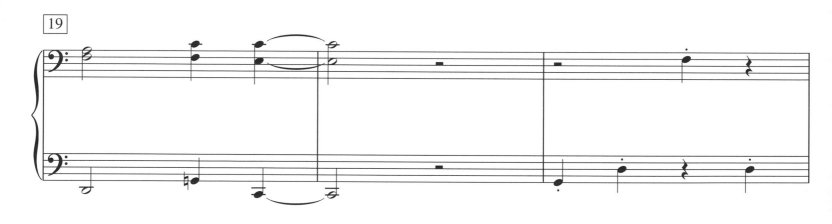

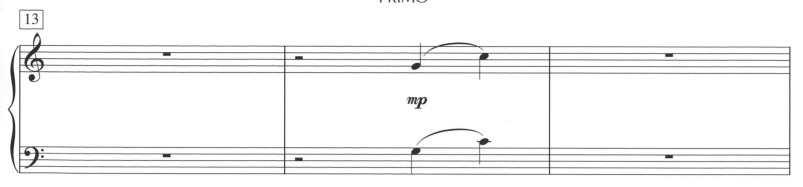

SECONDO

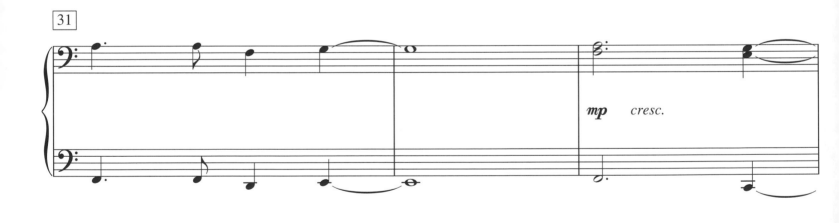

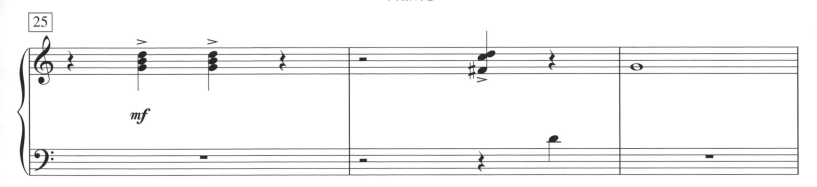

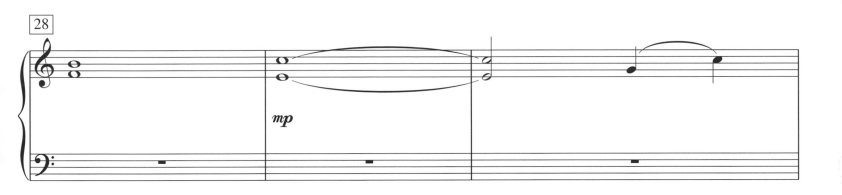

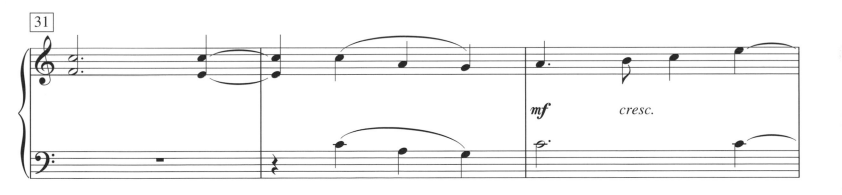

Piano For Two
A Variety of Piano Duets from Hal Leonard

I – BROADWAY DUETS
9 duet arrangements of Broadway favorites, including: Cabaret • Comedy Tonight • Ol' Man River • One • and more.

00292077 ....$10.95

LI – BROADWAY FAVORITES
A show-stopping collection of 8 songs arranged as piano duets. Includes: I Dreamed a Dream • If Ever I Would Leave You • Memory • People.

00290185 ....$9.95

LI – COLLECTED SACRED CLASSICS
Arranged by Bill Boyd
8 classics for piano duet, including: Ave Maria • A Mighty Fortress • Hallelujah from *Messiah* • and more.

00221009..........................$9.95

I – DISNEY DUETS
8 songs: Candle on the Water • Colors of the Wind • Cruella de Vil • Hakuna Matata • Someday • A Spoonful of Sugar • Winnie the Pooh • Zip-A-Dee-Doo-Dah.

00290484 ....$10.95

LI – DISNEY MOVIE HITS FOR TWO
9 fun favorites, including: Be Our Guest • Circle of Life • Friend like Me • Under the Sea • A Whole New World • and more.

00292076 ....$12.95

LI – DUET CLASSICS FOR PIANO
8 classical melodies, arranged as piano duets. Includes: Liebestraum (Liszt) • Minuet In G (Beethoven) • Sleeping Beauty Waltz (Tchaikovsky) • and more.

00290172 ....$6.95

LI – GERSHWIN PIANO DUETS
These duet arrangements of 10 Gershwin classics such as "I Got Plenty of Nuttin'," "Summertime," "It Ain't Necessarily So," and "Love Walked In" sound as full and satisfying as the orchestral originals.

00312603 ....$9.95

I – GREAT MOVIE THEMES
8 movie hits, including: Chariots of Fire • Colors of the Wind • The Entertainer • *Forrest Gump –* Main Title • Theme from *Jurassic Park* • Somewhere in Time • Somewhere, My Love • *Star Trek® – The Motion Picture* • and more.

00290494 ....$9.95

UI – LOVE DUETS
7 songs: All I Ask of You • Can You Feel the Love Tonight • Can't Help Falling in Love • Here, There, and Everywhere • Unchained Melody • When I Fall in Love • A Whole New World (Aladdin's Theme).

00290485 ....$8.95

LI – ANDREW LLOYD WEBBER PIANO DUETS
arr. Ann Collins
8 easy piano duets, featuring some of Andrew Lloyd Webber's biggest hits such as: All I Ask of You • Don't Cry for Me Argentina • Memory • I Don't Know How to Love Him.

00290332 ....$10.95

I – MOVIE DUETS
9 songs, including: Chariots of Fire • *The Godfather* (Love Theme) • *Romeo and Juliet* (Love Theme) • Theme from *Schindler's List* • and more.

00292078 ....$9.95

UI – COLE PORTER PIANO DUETS
What a better way to play these 6 Cole Porter love songs such as "Do I Love You?" "I Love Paris," "In The Still of the Night," than with a partner?

00312680.............................$9.95

UI – ROCK 'N' ROLL – PIANO DUETS
Ten early rock classics, including: Blue Suede Shoes • Don't Be Cruel • Rock Around the Clock • Shake, Rattle and Roll.

00290171.............................$9.95

LI – RODGERS & HAMMERSTEIN EASY PIANO DUETS
arr. Ann Collins
8 delightful easy piano duets, including: Do-Re-Mi • Edelweiss • My Favorite Things • Shall We Dance? • and more.

00290327...$8.95

I – THE SOUND OF MUSIC
9 songs, including: Do-Re-Mi • Edelweiss • My Favorite Things • The Sound of Music • and more.

00290389 ....$10.95

GRADING

LI = Lower Intermediate
I = Intermediate
UI = Upper Intermediate

FOR MORE INFORMATION, SEE YOUR LOCAL MUSIC DEALER, OR WRITE TO:

HAL•LEONARD CORPORATION
7777 W. BLUEMOUND RD. P.O. BOX 13819 MILWAUKEE, WI 53213